W9-DAO-505

HowToMean
Business

A pocket guide to more success at work

Scott Delman

Copyright ©1994 Client*Keep* Inc.

Unauthorized duplication prohibited.

All rights reserved, including the right to reproduce this book or portions thereof in any form, by any means, electronic or mechanical, including photocopying and recording, or by any storage or retrieval system, excepting brief quotes used in connection with reviews, without permission in writing from ClientKeep Inc.

Copyright © 1994 ClientKeep Inc.

Published by ClientKeep Inc., P.O. Box 665, Shelburne, VT 05482-0665

Second Edition, September 1995

Library of Congress Catalog Card Number: 95-92023
Delman, Scott
How To Mean Business
by Scott Delman
ISBN: 0-9645063-9-4

Orders and Inquiries: (800) 974-5337
Fax: (802) 985-5656

Edited by Andrew Yavelow, Hinesburg, VT.
Designed by DeskTop Prose, Shelburne, VT.
Printed in USA by Queen City Printers Inc., Burlington, VT.

Printed on recycled paper with soy-based inks.

Thanks to my family and friends and all of you who were so generous with your time and support.

Table of Contents

HowToMean Business

What's in it for you.

Do you want more success, fulfillment, and recognition at work?

Of course you do – everyone does. But too few people will ever get them. Why? Because in the hectic rush of a busy workday, it's simple human nature to lose sight of the basics. Sometimes, we just *forget* the fundamentals of what we're supposed to be doing and how we're supposed to be doing it. And as a result, we become scattered, frustrated, *even* ineffective.

But *How To Mean Business* helps you change that.

How To Mean Business is a fast, easy-to-use reminder guide to today's 50 most important concepts of workplace effectiveness. It tells you *what* those 50 vital concepts are, *why* they're important, and *how* to implement them. And it applies to *all* levels of employees in *all* types of businesses. It's good, straightforward business sense, presented in a simple, quick-reading reference format.

Here's how to use it.

Read through the book completely – each concept is just one page long, and takes less than a minute to read. Highlight the concepts and passages that seem most interesting and important, and if you have additional thoughts, make notes in the blank space.

Then, when you face a tough situation at work, refer back to these highlighted pages, concentrating especially on the "What to Do" sections. These reminders are likely to be exactly what you need. And if they're not, check the index – or just flip through the book – and find the concepts that do apply.

Many people find it helpful to read through *How To Mean Business* not just once, but regularly. Some people like to keep it in front of them as they work. Others like to start each day by reading a new page.

How To Mean Business can also be an effective starting point for discussions with your co-workers and managers. The concepts and implementation ideas here aren't just for you – they can be useful for your entire organization.

It Works!

You already know how good it feels to do your best work. Reading and using *How To Mean Business* will help you work at your best more and more often. You will work smarter, more enthusiastically, and more effectively. To put it simply, using *How To Mean Business* will help you become happier and more successful in your job. And in the process, you'll be helping your entire company.

Remember, you already have the knowledge and the skills. Let *How To Mean Business* help you use them more fully – and give yourself the satisfaction, the recognition, and the rewards of doing the best job you possibly can.

Scott Delman, president
Client*Keep Inc.*

HowToMean
Business

Business Principles

These concepts are fundamental to the daily operation of every business. When you remember and use them, you will strengthen your personal effectiveness and the integrity of your company.

1. **Your Company** ... is a mutual dependency

2. **The Workplace** ... is *your* work area

3. **Your Manager** ... needs your cooperation

4. **Co-Workers** ... are your business partners

5. **Your Marketplace** ... is unlimited

6. **Reputations** ... endure

7. **Client Retention** ... is your business

8. **Quality** ... comes from you

9. **Compete** ... to win

10. **Survey** ... then you will know

11. **Trends** ... are undeniable

12. **Reports** ... point the way

13. **Profits** ... are for you

14. **The Bottom Line** ... is a company's value

Your Company

... is a mutual dependency

Your Company

definition

Your Company is the organization that pays you in exchange for your support. Each of you is dependent on the other.

what to do

See your company as a community. Devote yourself to its ongoing health and growth by understanding your role and performing at your full potential. Treat every one of your co-workers with appreciation and respect. Behave proactively, supportively, and responsibly.

why to do it

Everything you do at work affects your company. By performing your job with skill and a positive attitude, you create a more desirable work environment and help your company project a more successful image; your work life – and the work life of everyone around you – becomes more meaningful.

remember

Only a successful company can provide jobs for its workers.

HowToMean
Business

The Workplace

... is *your* work area

The Workplace

definition

Your Workplace is the location, building, office area, machinery, equipment, and emotional environment in, with, and around which you work every day.

what to do

Contribute to the kind of workplace that *you* value. Treat every co-worker like a client, and every client like a friend – with honesty, sincerity, and respect. Do excellent work, and speak highly of your peers and company. Cooperate, show you care, and be responsible for your own actions. Work within company guidelines, be neat and clean, and always work safely.

why to do it

When every worker contributes to a good workplace, work quality is higher, and productivity and profits go up. Teamwork is stronger and your company becomes a more stable and enjoyable place to work.

remember

A good workplace is like a good home – supportive, safe, and well worth investing in.

HowToMean
Business

Your Manager

... needs your cooperation

Your Manager

definition

Your Manager is the person who provides and facilitates your job, and is responsible for everything you do in the workplace.

what to do

For the best results, *team up* with your manager. Contribute your best by approaching your work proactively, responding positively to training opportunities, and being punctual with assignments. Communicate, cooperate, and allow your manager to help you. And, when appropriate, express your appreciation.

why to do it

You and your manager depend on each other for success; your job is to do good work, and your manager's job is to help that happen. When you and your manager communicate effectively and work together, your work environment becomes more pleasant, more productive, and more rewarding. You, your manager, and your company will all be more successful.

remember

Cooperating with your manager helps you **both** *become more valuable employees.*

HowToMean
Business

Co-Workers

... are your business partners

Co-Workers

definition

Your Co-Workers are all the other people who work at your company. Each one of you has an impact on all the others.

what to do

Treat co-workers as your work family: with courtesy, respect, and support. Help them succeed at their jobs, and give co-workers the same high level of commitment, work, and service that you give your *clients*.

why to do it

The quality of your work life and the success of your company are entirely up to you and your co-workers. When you help each other, you help yourselves.

remember

Together, you and your co-workers make your company succeed.

HowToMean
Business

Your Marketplace

... is unlimited

Your Marketplace

definition

Your Marketplace is the area in which you sell, and in which your clients and prospective customers buy. Its only boundaries are those imposed by you and your ability to communicate.

what to do

Your marketplace should be protected, developed, and expanded. Protect it by providing better products and service than your competitors. Develop and expand it through prospecting, marketing, and self-promotion.

why to do it

Success breeds success. Being visible, proactive, and successful in your existing marketplace reassures your clients that doing business with you is the right decision. It helps you gain new customers and enhance your company's profits.

remember

Your marketplace can extend as far as your company can reach.

Reputations

... endure

Reputations

definition

Your Reputation is what other people say about you, your company, its products, or its service. People in your marketplace know you by reputation – even *before* they do business with you.

what to do

Believe in your work, do it well, and be proud of what you do. Speak highly of your company and co-workers, and ask your clients to spread the good word about doing business with you.

why to do it

A good reputation is one of the most powerful marketing devices of all: it brings in many clients, creates positive expectations, and leads to much profitable business.

remember

A good reputation brings in business; a bad one keeps it away.

HowToMean
Business

Client Retention

... is your business

Client Retention

definition

Client Retention means continuing to do business with the clients you have.

what to do

To retain your clients, you must out-perform your competitors in service, product quality, value, ethics, and professionalism. It helps to remember that your clients provide your paycheck. Stay in touch with them. Ask them for suggestions about how you can improve – then do it. Do *more* than your clients expect. And above all, be sure to thank them.

why to do it

Retaining your clients makes your daily business operations more predictable and easier to manage. It requires less work and less expense to retain existing clients than it does to replace lost ones – and it's far more profitable.

remember

A client who stays has value; a client who strays has none.

Quality

... comes from you

Quality

definition

Quality is the inherent integrity, reliability, and value of your products and service.

what to do

Create and maintain the highest possible quality in your products and service. Constantly evaluate them, and make sure that ongoing adjustments are part of your business plan. Stay alert: notice and communicate all opportunities for improvement.

why to do it

Clients expect and deserve superior quality. When you give your clients the best, they remain satisfied and loyal – and your company's overall strength and potential for growth are enhanced.

remember

Great quality satisfies your clients – and thwarts your competitors.

Compete

... to win

Compete

definition

Competing is trying to be better, more efficient, and more effective than anyone else who does what you do.

what to do

The contest begins *within yourself*; be the absolute best you personally can be. Set the highest realistic standards and goals for yourself. Behave professionally, communicate effectively, and provide great customer service. Be persistent and visualize the winning results you expect.

why to do it

When you perform in a focused and competitive manner, you challenge yourself, expand your abilities, and produce the best results. With the best results, you'll earn the greatest rewards, and leave your competitors behind.

remember

*To win in business, you must **out-perform** those who are trying to improve on what you do.*

HowToMean
Business

Survey

... then you will know

Survey

definition

To Survey is to gather and examine information from your clients and the marketplace about the perception of your company, its products, or its performance.

what to do

Develop and implement a plan for systematically obtaining feedback, ideas, and suggestions from clients, consumers, co-workers, and others working in your industry and related fields. Interpret and analyze your findings. Then take steps – proactively – to improve on existing conditions, and prepare for the future.

why to do it

Business conditions change continually. Surveys provide information for coping with and anticipating change: they help you make adjustments that minimize losses and maximize opportunities. Surveys help you operate with more control, and limit unwanted risk.

remember

Not surveying for information is a gamble: you can try your luck, but the odds are stacked against you.

HowToMean
Business

Trends

... are undeniable

Trends

definition

Trends are changes that can be measured or predicted in the performance of a person, company, or marketplace.

what to do

Measure your work performance regularly, and analyze how it is trending. When you see a trend in the right direction, be certain to support it. When you see a trend in the wrong direction, make appropriate corrections *immediately*.

why to do it

Small changes now can have huge impact over the long term. By discovering trends early and making immediate small adjustments, you maximize opportunities and avoid having to make more difficult corrections when it may be too late.

remember

Keep an eye on the trends, and you'll never be confronted with big surprises.

HowToMean
Business

Reports

... point the way

Reports

definition

Reports document the status of your business. They provide data you can analyze and use to spot trends.

what to do

Observe, document, and track every key aspect of your basic business activities; whenever possible, do it with numbers. Chart your progress, and analyze the results to identify trends in your business performance. Correct potential problems by making appropriate changes as soon as possible.

why to do it

When generated on a regular basis, reports allow you to inspect the elements of your business and document your progress. They help you discover problems early, when they are easiest to correct and when corrections will have the greatest long-term impact.

remember

Reports are the road map of work; they show where you've been, and where you are going.

Profits

... are for you

Profits

definition

Profits are the measurable financial gains that exist *only* when earnings exceed expenses.

what to do

Your job is to serve your clients at a profit to your company; to provide your clients with the best products and service in exchange for the best profit. Minimize expenses by working efficiently, reducing waste, and conserving resources.

why to do it

Profits allow your company to exist, and are the source of your paycheck. By doing everything you can to contribute to profits, you help give your company – and your job – a future.

remember

For your job to continue, your company **must** *make a profit.*

The Bottom Line

... is a company's value

The Bottom Line

definition

The Bottom Line is the amount of profit (or loss) a business makes overall – the dollars-and-cents accounting of total income and expenses.

what to do

To strengthen the overall bottom line, all employees must maximize the profitability of every element of the business. Each must work efficiently, use supplies and materials effectively, conserve energy resources, and look for ways to reduce costs.

why to do it

A business is only as strong as each of it component parts. For a company and its workers to earn the largest profits, every element of the business must be efficient and effective.

remember

When the bottom line improves, everybody profits.

HowToMean
Business

Client Relation Skills

These concepts are fundamental to how you interact with clients. When you remember and use them, you will make your client relationships more enduring, more reliable, and more profitable.

15. **Customers** ... pay your wage

16. **Clients** ... are for keeping

17. **Client Erosion** ... costs you money

18. **Customer Service** ... matters

19. **Effective Communication** ... reaches your target

20. **Follow Up** ... to stay in control

21. **Feedback** ... tells it like it is

22. **Customer Satisfaction** ... means success

23. **Client Loyalty** ... is up to you

24. **Thank You** ... is more than words

HowToMean
Business

Customers

... pay your wage

Customers

definition

Customers are buyers who purchase your company's products or services for the first time. When they buy repeatedly, customers become *clients*.

what to do

If you think of each customer as providing your paycheck, every customer's importance immediately becomes clear. Your goal is to turn every customer into a repeat-business client. To do that, you must provide every customer with top-notch treatment from the moment you meet – even *before* they buy.

why to do it

Your opportunity to create a long-term business relationship with your customers begins before the first sale – even before they measure the value of your product or service. It begins with your first contact, when they decide how they feel about doing business with *you*.

remember

Dissatisfied customers take their business elsewhere. And part of your paycheck goes with them.

Clients

... are for keeping

Clients

definition

Clients are customers who decide to do business with you repeatedly. A relationship has developed – it must be actively and professionally maintained.

what to do

If you think of your clients as you do your friends, your willingness to help them will become automatic. Treat them with kindness and respect as you maintain ongoing contact, follow up on purchases, and ask for feedback and referrals. Above all, keep *their* best interests in mind.

why to do it

Clients do business with people who make them feel good. Clients are looking for pleasurable, productive, profitable, long-lasting relationships.

remember

Your good relationship with your client is the hardest thing for a competitor to outdo.

HowToMean
Business

Client Erosion

... costs you money

Client Erosion

definition

Client Erosion is a shrinkage in your number of clients. It means your business is going in the wrong direction.

what to do

To minimize client erosion, give your clients *more* of what they expect. Operate more professionally, and with more integrity. Provide better service. Outdo your competition. Do everything you can to enhance your client relationships (and in the process, you'll enhance the reputation of your company). If clients stop doing business with you, talk with them and find out why – then make appropriate changes. Actively prospect for new clients.

why to do it

Replacing lost clients is harder, more expensive, and far less profitable than keeping the clients you already have.

remember

It's easier to keep clients happy than it is to change their minds once they decide to leave.

Customer Service

... matters

Customer Service

definition

Customer Service is how you communicate with your clients as people, meet their needs and expectations, and keep your word. It means supporting your clients in the ways that satisfy them.

what to do

Serve each client "givingly," by adopting *their* best interests as *your* best interests. Appear happy to help, be proactive, and always do more than your clients expect. Leave nothing half-done – see every task through to successful completion.

why to do it

The quality of customer service is measured entirely by the client. Clients who receive great service will be more satisfied with your company and its products, happier with their decision to do business with you, and more likely to buy from you again. They'll also be far more cooperative in solving problems that arise.

remember

The only customer service that helps your business is **great** *customer service.*

Effective Communication

... reaches your target

Effective Communication

definition

Effective Communication occurs when your message is received and understood. It has two parts: the *content* of the message, and the way your client *feels* about you and the way you deliver it.

what to do

Speak to all your clients in terms they understand; listen and respond sincerely. Ask questions, maintain eye contact, be patient and still. Speak their names, smile, be friendly and straightforward. If you have a genuine interest in your clients, *you* will become the reason they want to do business with your company.

why to do it

Effective communication gets your message across clearly and paves the way for successful business transactions and relationships. It makes clients feel comfortable, and is vital for client retention. Ineffective communication limits transactions and relationships to less than their full potential value.

remember

Effective communication delivers the message to your client; ineffective communication delivers your client to your competitor.

Follow Up

... to stay in control

Follow Up

definition

Following Up is maintaining ongoing communication with your clients after the initial contact or sale. It's the best tactic for effective customer service, client retention, and prospecting.

what to do

Follow up *frequently* after each sale, making sure that each contact is made for a specific reason, and to accomplish a specific goal. For example, contact your clients to request an evaluation of your product or service, to seek referrals, or to thank them.

why to do it

Your clients measure the quality of your business relationship. By following up and communicating regularly, you reassure them that working with *you* continues to be the right business choice.

remember

Your clients are often contacted by your competitors; shouldn't they hear more often from **you**?

HowToMean
Business

Feedback

... tells it like it is

Feedback

definition

Feedback is another person's assessment or response to what you do. Getting feedback is necessary for monitoring and strengthening your progress.

what to do

Ask people what they think – and they will tell you. *Listen* to what they say as objectively as possible, and analyze the information. Then, use what you learn to make whatever adjustments are appropriate.

why to do it

Business conditions and directions change continually; feedback gives you the information you need to stay on the right track. What's more, clients, co-workers, and others respect you when you ask for feedback. Asking people their opinions – and listening to the responses – strengthens the bonds between you.

remember

Doing business without feedback is like flying blind without a compass: you're likely to head in the wrong direction.

Customer Satisfaction

... means success

Customer Satisfaction

definition

True Customer Satisfaction occurs when your customer is sincerely pleased with you, your company, your products, and your service.

what to do

Imagine that you come to work just to help each individual customer. Be gracious and sincere, and support your customer in the ways he or she needs. If you remember that everything you do to please your customer ultimately contributes to your paycheck, you'll want to do even *more* than the customer expects.

why to do it

When your customers are satisfied, they keep doing business with you. As their satisfaction increases, they become more and more trusting. Future transactions become easier, and working with them becomes more enjoyable and more rewarding.

remember

*If your customers are satisfied, it means that **you** are doing your job well.*

Client Loyalty

... is up to you

Client Loyalty

definition

Client Loyalty is a faithful, powerful allegiance to you, your company, its products, and its service. Loyal clients are easier to serve and satisfy.

what to do

Build loyalty by delivering great service in whatever way is most meaningful to each client. Be sincere, patient, helpful, and friendly. And always do business with total integrity.

why to do it

Loyal clients provide greater financial rewards for your company; they create a strong base of business, and help ensure your paycheck. When you know that you have truly helped your clients and nurtured their loyalty, everything about your work feels more worthwhile.

remember

*Client loyalty is built over time; it is maintained by the work **you** do.*

Thank You

... is more than words

Thank You

definition

Thank You is a sincere expression of heartfelt appreciation.

what to do

When you thank someone, make eye contact, smile, and let your feelings of warmth and gratitude clearly come through.

why to do it

Before almost anything else, people evaluate how they *feel* about doing business with you. When you give a sincere thank you, you make someone feel good: they get the message that you appreciate their actions – and the feeling that you appreciate *them*. An insincere thank you, on the other hand, feels like a dismissal, and gives the message "good-bye."

remember

Say thank you when you mean it, and mean it when you say it.

Productivity Builders

These concepts are fundamental to greater efficiency and effectiveness. When you remember and use them, you will improve your overall productivity and the quality of your work.

25. **Training** ... is your opportunity to grow

26. **Simplify** ... and get more done

27. **The Telephone** ... gets your message across

28. **Punctuality** ... says you care

29. **Delegate** ... to accomplish more

30. **Proactivity** ... puts you in control, and moves you ahead

31. **Prospecting** ... pays

32. **Selling** ... is based on relationships

33. **Buying Decisions** ... are your clients' solutions

34. **Closing the Sale** ... earns you the prize

35. **Referrals** ... are your easiest sales

Training

... is your opportunity to grow

Training

definition

Training is the process that helps you perform with more understanding and greater expertise. Training gives you information, skill, experience, and wisdom. It is the activity that enables you to improve and grow.

what to do

Participate in the appropriate training opportunities that are offered to you, and request more as you feel the need. Approach each training session with an open mind and the determination to apply your new knowledge.

why to do it

Training is a *privilege*, the surest way to enhance your work and advance yourself. It allows you to demonstrate your best intentions and display your full worth.

remember

Workers with training deserve and get more of what they want.

Simplify

... and get more done

Simplify

definition

To Simplify a task is to make it easier by breaking it down into small, manageable steps.

what to do

Identify the steps necessary to complete a large or complex task. One at a time, accomplish each step in productive sequence. Stay disciplined and focused on whichever step you're on, but always keep your desired final outcome in mind.

why to do it

Large challenges can be overwhelming, but when you reduce seemingly huge tasks to simpler components, you'll see that you *can* get each aspect of the job done right. You'll feel more self-confident, versatile, and skilled. You'll become significantly more productive.

remember

Even the most complex task is simply a series of smaller steps.

HowToMean
Business

The Telephone

... gets your message across

The Telephone

definition

The Telephone is a powerful and readily accessible communication tool. Use it skillfully, and you can gather and distribute information, make sales, and service your clients.

what to do

When you're on the phone, listen to the other person, ask questions, and respond sincerely with the intention of being helpful. It's important to feel and *sound* warm; smiling as you speak will help you do that.

why to do it

People like to be listened to and appreciated. The better you listen and the friendlier you sound on the telephone, the more likely you'll be to receive cooperation and good results.

remember

Poor telephone communication is like a bad connection: your message never gets through.

HowToMean
Business

Punctuality

... says you care

Punctuality

definition

Punctuality means being physically and *attitudinally* on time and prepared. It is a habit of successful people.

what to do

Arrive at work early enough to prepare yourself for the day. Plan how you can best help your company and clients, set your work goals, and begin on time. Be punctual for all meetings, appointments, and deadlines.

why to do it

Being punctual demonstrates respect for your co-workers and clients, and pride in yourself. Completing your assignments punctually contributes to efficient output. You will be noticed, appreciated, and rewarded for your dependability and good attitude; others will follow. You and your entire company will benefit.

remember

Being punctual demonstrates your commitment to your company's success.

Delegate

... to accomplish more

Delegate

definition

When you Delegate, you assign a task to someone else, while maintaining responsibility for its successful completion.

what to do

Assign people tasks they are capable of accomplishing. Give people clear, detailed instructions of what you expect, and be *certain* they understand. Then support them as needed and be available to guide them.

why to do it

When you delegate successfully, you greatly increase your own output – while allowing others to gain experience, confidence, and self-esteem.

remember

When you delegate, you free your time, accomplish more, and help other workers grow.

HowToMean
Business

Proactivity

... puts you in control, and
moves you ahead

Proactivity

definition

Proactivity is the creative process of anticipating, planning ahead and controlling a situation. The opposite of proactivity – reactivity – is reacting to a situation that's already out of your control.

what to do

Anticipate what's likely to happen next. Be creative, and imagine all the different actions you could take to affect that situation – and what the results of each possible action would be. Then choose and implement the action that will give you the results you want.

why to do it

When you keep the future impact of your actions in mind, it's easier to get good results – because the results are within your control. For example, workloads are always easiest to handle when you manage them with forethought.

remember

*When you are aware of **all** the possibilities, it's easier to manage the outcome.*

Prospecting

... pays

Prospecting

definition

Prospecting is increasing your business by proactively seeking out new customers and opportunities.

what to do

Do your work in a way that makes you proud, and tell people about it. Develop a realistic prospecting plan and follow it *faithfully*. Contact prospects consistently in ways appropriate to your company, and ask them to do business with you when they become ready.

why to do it

Actively prospecting allows you to reach more buyers, earn more sales, be more productive, and use your time efficiently during slow periods.

remember

Prospecting isn't nearly as hard as waiting around for something to do.

Selling

... is based on relationships

Selling

definition

Selling means creating a willingness in your client to buy *from you*.

what to do

Selling involves more than just your company's tangible products or service. It involves how your client *feels* about the way you do business together. To sell effectively, you must provide professional behavior and service, ask questions, listen, and focus on satisfying your client's needs.

why to do it

Every client's preference is to do business where they feel comfortable, understood, and important. Offering that sort of business relationship is the most important sale of all.

remember

Your successful relationships with clients will create sales for your company.

HowToMean
Business

Buying Decisions

... are your clients' solutions

Buying Decisions

definition

Buying Decisions are the choices to purchase. They're made when a client's buying criteria are satisfactorily met.

what to do

If you can demonstrate that your product will satisfy your client's needs, then your client will buy. Help your clients *identify* their needs: what they want, why they want it, how they will use it, how it will help them, and how having it will make them feel. Then show them how your product or service *satisfies* those needs.

why to do it

People buy for *their* reasons, not yours. Until they know clearly what those reasons are – and how your product addresses them – they will not buy from you. When they do know clearly, buying decisions are more easily and appropriately made.

remember

An appropriate buying decision makes a client happy; an inappropriate one can be a lingering problem.

HowToMean
Business

Closing the Sale

... earns you the prize

Closing the Sale

definition

Closing the Sale is when you ask your customer to reach a final buying decision. To do it successfully, you must gain clarity and agreement from the customer through every step of the sales process.

what to do

Begin the selling process by establishing rapport. Ask the customer what his or her needs are, and *listen* to the response. Describe the ways your product will satisfy this customer's needs, and finally ask them to buy from you. Address objections, and again ask the customer to buy.

why to do it

Asking customers to buy from you is the key to closing sales. Establishing open rapport with customers makes the asking easy and natural; creating the opportunity to ask several times increases your chance of success.

remember

Closing the sale helps your customer, your company, and yourself.

Referrals

... are your easiest sales

Referrals

definition

A Referral is a potential customer who is recommended to you or your company by another person.

what to do

Follow up with your clients by asking them for referrals on a regular basis; if you have earned your clients' respect and trust, they will help you. Always contact the referrals whose names you receive, and always thank the clients who referred them to you.

why to do it

Doing business with referrals makes your job easier: referred customers are more trusting, cooperative, and quicker to purchase than customers whom you have not yet met. Referrals help you and your company build and maintain a strong client base.

remember

Favorable referrals deliver business; unfavorable ones drive it away.

HowToMean
Business

Skills for Growth

These concepts are fundamental to your personal attitude and performance. When you remember and use them, you will make yourself a better co-worker, and a stronger and more valuable employee.

36. **Professionalism** ... is about standards

37. **Motivation** ... is the true reason within

38. **Goals** ... give you purpose

39. **A Personal Mission Statement** ... reflects your standards

40. **Self-Confidence** ... lets you reach your potential

41. **Perseverance** ... keeps you moving ahead

42. **Growth** ... promotes progress

43. **Rapport** ... creates successful relationships

44. **Ask Questions** ... and get answers

45. **Advice** ... is information to welcome and consider

46. **Honesty** ... pays big dividends

47. **Excel** ... and step ahead

48. **Experience** ... is the reward for time and effort

49. **Success** ... means you've done it right

50. **Smile** ... it's an international language

HowToMean
Business

Professionalism

... is about standards

Professionalism

definition

Professionalism means maintaining the *highest standards* of quality and ethics. A professional is knowledgeable, skilled, experienced, and up-to-date.

what to do

Always work at your best level. Keep current with all the new developments and information that are pertinent to your profession, train regularly, and improve constantly.

why to do it

Clients choose to do business with those who consistently deliver the highest-quality products and service in the most professional manner. Keep *your* standards at their peak, and your clients will continue to be satisfied.

remember

Professionalism is your strongest contribution to your company's continued good name.

HowToMean
Business

Motivation

... is the true reason within

Motivation

definition

Your Motivation is what causes you to do what you do.

what to do

Do you work to make lots of money, help others, support a family, win praise, feel successful, take vacations...? Think about *why* you stay at this job; figure out what's really in it *for you*.

why to do it

Motivation guides your actions. By understanding what your motivation is, and by doing your job well, you can work more directly for what you truly want.

remember

*Motivation gives you the **power** to perform.*

HowToMean
Business

Goals

... give you purpose

Goals

definition

Goals are what you set out to accomplish: clear visions with measurable attainment.

what to do

Decide exactly what you want to accomplish, and understand why. Outline a plan of small, simple steps you can take to accomplish your goals. Complete each step in turn. Be flexible enough to adjust for unforeseen problems or new information – but always work toward your ultimate goals.

why to do it

Goals give you a sense of purpose and power – because *you* choose them. Moving toward your goals in a series of small steps makes it easier for you to succeed, and easier to measure your progress; it allows you to savor the pride and satisfaction of your accomplishments along the way.

remember

If you don't pursue goals, you'll always be where you are right now.

HowToMean
Business

A Personal Mission Statement

... reflects your standards

A Personal Mission Statement

definition

A Personal Mission Statement describes the values, morals, and ethical standards you bring to your job.

what to do

Become aware of your reasons, motivations, and goals for working, and the standards by which you measure yourself. Write them all down. This is your personal mission statement. Look at it regularly, and remember why you're there.

why to do it

Having a personal mission statement helps you stay focused on your objectives and on what "doing a good job" means *for you*. It can give you the strength and clarity to get through difficult times on the job.

remember

Understanding what's important to you keeps you headed in the right direction.

HowToMean
Business

Self-Confidence

... lets you reach your
potential

Self-Confidence

definition

Self-Confidence is the knowledge that you *can* do what you choose to do.

what to do

Believe in your ability to handle what comes your way, and then reach for what you want. Re-read your personal mission statement, and take risks with the assurance that you *are* a strong, intelligent, and capable person.

why to do it

Your mind is your most powerful ally: *believing* that you can succeed allows you the opportunity to succeed. No matter what the outcome of your risk-taking, you'll gain information and experience, and keep moving forward.

remember

With self-confidence, every challenge is an opportunity to look forward to.

HowToMean
Business

Perseverance

... keeps you moving ahead

Perseverance

definition

Perseverance means continuing toward your goals despite difficulties and opposition.

what to do

Clearly identify your motivation and the goals you want to reach. Create a plan of simple steps to get you there, and complete each step in turn; change strategies as the need arises. Understand that overcoming discouragement is part of the process, and *keep going anyway.*

why to do it

With perseverance, you'll accomplish far more than the average worker. You'll discover that even the most difficult tasks can be completed successfully.

remember

If you persevere, you'll most often reach your goal.

Growth

... promotes progress

Growth

definition

Growth in an individual allows the expansion of skills, confidence, experience, output, and self-esteem. Growth in a company allows the expansion of goals, market share, profits, reputation, and recognition.

what to do

The decision to grow personally – to improve – is entirely within your power. Set new goals for yourself, then persevere and work hard to achieve them. Look for new opportunities to learn, and accept new challenges.

why to do it

Growing as an individual – learning and accomplishing more – strengthens your pride and self-esteem. You become more valuable to yourself, and that increases your value to those around you. Rewards are sure to follow.

remember

A company can only grow as fast as the individuals who work there.

HowToMean
Business

Rapport

... creates successful
relationships

Rapport

definition

Rapport is a mutually clear and comfortable feeling between two people; good rapport means a relationship is in harmony.

what to do

First, be open and giving of yourself. Then, focus on the person you're communicating with, and help them feel important: maintain eye contact, smile, listen, and be patient. Appreciate people for who they are, and care about what they have to say. Be willing to look at things from *their* point of view.

why to do it

Establishing rapport makes communication easier, more trusting, flexible, dependable, and productive. Enhancing rapport strengthens relationships, and encourages more ambitious and substantial accomplishments.

remember

Rapport allows people to move together toward their goals.

Ask Questions

... and get answers

Ask Questions

definition

Asking Questions is the way to gain information and the understanding necessary to create solutions.

what to do

Ask open-ended questions in a pleasant, direct manner; listen non-judgmentally to the responses. People will tell you what you want and need to know.

why to do it

When you ask people questions, you demonstrate that you care about them and what they have to say. You help them feel good about themselves – and about you. Asking questions of your clients and co-workers helps you establish rapport, and strengthens your relationships; it's also the best way to learn exactly how to help people most effectively.

remember

Asking questions is the first step to greater wisdom.

HowToMean
Business

Advice

... is information to welcome
and consider

Advice

definition

Advice is a recommendation about an event, a condition, or an issue.

what to do

If your goal is to improve, advice is a strong ally. Consider *all* advice as valuable. Seek it out, listen with an open mind – and then make your own decisions.

why to do it

There are often several "right" ways to solve a problem. When you seek advice, you receive information and solutions you might not have thought of yourself. The more advice you get, the better your chances of finding and choosing the best solutions.

remember

Gathering advice helps you discover new possibilities.

HowToMean
Business

Honesty

... pays big dividends

Honesty

definition

Honesty means being completely truthful – not trying to take advantage by giving partial information or being deceptive.

what to do

Keep the best interests of your client in mind, and be fair and honorable in all your dealings and transactions. Give your client all of the pertinent information – whether you are asked for it or not. Deliver everything you promise.

why to do it

When you are honest, you never have to hide from your clients or yourself. You gain the personal pride of knowing that you work with integrity. You gain the professional satisfaction of knowing that your clients can and do trust you. And you and your company gain the profits of well-founded, long-lasting business relationships.

remember

Honesty builds the most dependable and successful relationships.

Excel

... and step ahead

Excel

definition

To Excel means to out-perform yourself.

what to do

Learn more and do more. Search out ways to work smarter, more efficiently, faster, and more effectively. Approach your work with more pride and integrity. Do it *better* than you ever have before.

why to do it

The effort to excel helps you grow, feel better about yourself, and be worth more to your company. You'll gain notice and recognition – and, in time, more personal and professional rewards.

remember

The effort to excel rewards itself.

HowToMean
Business

Experience

... is the reward for time
and effort

Experience

definition

Experience is the familiarity, knowledge, and wisdom you gain with time.

what to do

Work hard to improve yourself and your performance, and make it your business to keep learning new things. Acknowledge and learn from all your accomplishments, and welcome the mistakes that teach you better ways.

why to do it

As you increase your familiarity, knowledge, and wisdom through experience, you'll be able to give more to your clients, your co-workers, and your company. Your increased value will be recognized and rewarded.

remember

Whether you succeed or fail, the experience you gain is always worthwhile.

Success

... means you've done it right

Success

definition

Success is when you accomplish a goal that you've set for yourself.

what to do

Set clear goals and objectives for yourself. Write them down, create step-by-step plans to accomplish them, and follow through with perseverance and flexibility. Then, when you've accomplished a goal or objective to your satisfaction, step back and enjoy the feeling of success. *Be proud* – you've earned it.

why to do it

Success is a measure of a job well done, and nothing feels better.

remember

Success is the fuel that powers your pride.

HowToMean
Business

Smile

... it's an international language

Smile

definition

A sincere Smile is when your lips curl up at the ends, your eyes get warm and relaxed, and you feel good inside.

what to do

When you interact with a client or a co-worker, imagine how pleased you'll feel when you help them. Now let those feelings shine through on your face, and be heard in your voice.

why to do it

A *sincere* smile opens the door to successful communication. It displays your good intentions, and puts other people at ease.

remember

Business transactions that end with a smile usually begin with one.

Index

HowToMean
Business